Create INFLUENCE

10 Ways to Impress and Guide Others

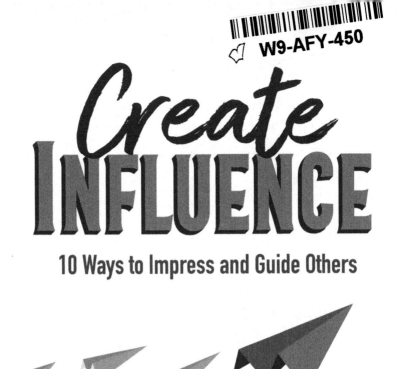

Keith & Tom "Big Al" Schreiter

Published by Fortune Network Publishing

PO Box 890084

Houston, TX 77289 USA

Telephone: +1 (281) 280-9800

BigAlBooks.com

ISBN-10: 1-948197-27-8

ISBN-13: 978-1-948197-27-4

CONTENTS

PREFACE

Want to change the world? Or at least be heard? No one wants to be just a footnote in other people's lives. We want to make a difference.

How does it feel when we are ignored? Not respected? Or not taken seriously? It feels frustrating, because we know we could contribute to conversations.

We want to be noticed. And we want influence so our contributions matter.

If we weren't born into a royal family or we aren't a movie star, then how do we get the influence we need so that our voice matters? We build it one step at a time.

This book contains ten simple and easy ways to get influence immediately. Anyone can perform these steps. We only have to choose to start.

Let's get ready to make a difference by creating influence.

INFLUENCE AND THE CANOE TRIP OF HORROR.

John Doe was a nobody. Invisible at work. Not respected by his friends. Few people looked at him when he ventured into public.

There was nothing wrong with John. He was a nice guy, but he blended in with the wallpaper. No one thought much of him. No one took notice when he spoke.

Like most of us, John wanted to share his dreams and ideas to change the lives of others. But to do that, he would need to command respect and possess the ability to have influence with others.

Feeling invisible is one of the worst feelings we can have. Everyone wants influence. Few of us know how to get it.

What does influence really mean?

Influence can have many definitions. But for now, let's say that influence means that others trust us and believe us <u>plus</u> ... they want to take action on what we say.

Here is an example of someone with influence.

A doctor gets excited about investing in real estate. She picks up the phone, calls her friends and says, "I believe real estate is a good investment for us now. Would you like to get involved in real estate with me?"

The reply from her friends?

"Of course. Here is my credit card number. Let's do it!"

This response came before any explanation of the future real estate investments. Why did the doctor's friends reply like this?

Because the doctor has influence.

But wait! This doctor has no expertise or previous investment experience. This doctor knows nothing about the real estate market.

There are many other real estate professionals, brokers, and investors with far more experience and knowledge. However, if these real estate professionals call these same friends, no one wants to invest. Her friends question the professionals about details, safety, and their concerns.

So, what was different about the doctor?

The doctor's friends trusted the doctor. A curious program takes over in human minds. The friends knew the doctor had high levels of expertise in medicine. The doctor directly gave them advice about health. Because the doctor was a high-level expert in health, they automatically gave the doctor their trust and belief in all other areas. We'll talk more about this program later.

Rapport means our prospects can trust and believe what we say.

Influence is so much more.

Influence means our prospects not only trust and believe us, but also respect what we say. And then they take action upon what we say.

The teacher's assistant.

The teacher's assistant has been in the community for 40 years. Yet, she does not have influence. Yes, she has rapport with people she talks to. She has their trust. But because she is not an expert in an area they respect, she doesn't have the influence needed to get people to act.

"Expertise" makes influence easier.

When someone has influence, we tend not to question the future. We feel that the future they describe will be okay.

The canoe trip of horror.

When I left school, I became a new employee at a large office. The person next to me always had new ideas. He was the first person to try something new. He came to the office with the latest ideas for health, recreation, and places to go for holidays. Everyone respected him because he took charge and was the first to volunteer for any project.

One day he came to work and said, "This Saturday there is a canoe race down the Des Plaines River. This could be a fun group outing for all of us."

Everyone, including me, chimed in, "Yes. Let's do it."

We agreed this would be an adventure we would relive at the coffee machine all next week. Our influencer arranged for canoe rentals. All we had to do was show up.

Now, had any of us been in a canoe before? No. But why should we worry? He told us this 26-mile canoe race would be easy. We didn't have to win. We just had to participate and have fun. How hard could this be? Two people in a canoe, going downstream in a river, what could go wrong? And to make things even easier, this was early spring when the river flooded with melted snow and the current would be extra fast. We would simply coast down this fast-flowing river.

What were we thinking???

Obviously not much.

With our beer-fortified confidence, many of us fell out of the canoe instantly. The water was freezing. Teamwork? Two amateur paddlers in an unbalanced canoe.

What could go wrong?

Everything.

Because the river was flooded, we couldn't guide the canoe. The floodwaters carried us into trees, cement dams, other canoes ... we were a floating disaster.

Life jackets saved the day. After several near-death experiences, we finished the race smelling like the dirty waters of the Des Plaines River. Frozen, smelly, exhausted ... what a great time!

On Monday morning, we stood by the coffee machine and relived our near-death experiences. And guess what?

We couldn't wait for the next suggestion from our influencer at work.

We want to be influencers.

We don't want to be like John Doe. We want to make a difference. We want to affect other people's lives.

Imagine our lives as influencers to others. We share our best ideas, and they say, "Yes! Let's do it!"

This doesn't have to be a dream. We can start building our influence now.

But how do we get the respect and influence?

Before we can get influence, we have to create rapport. Rapport means that others believe us and trust us. They accept that what we say is true. If we have to defend every statement we make, we will never get to the influence stage with others.

Yes, rapport comes first. Then we can build our influence on the solid foundation of belief and trust.

So, let's review some basic rapport skills first.

Getting rapport first.

First, a few examples of people that have rapport with us. We trust them and believe what they say to be true.

We live in a rural community. Another farmer, who everyone knows is honest, voices his opinion. We accept what this person says as true. His track record in our community makes it easy for us to believe, instead of doubt.

Our repair man serviced our appliances for 30 years. When he tells us about his experiences, we believe the experiences to be true. We don't think he would lie to us or take advantage of us. He has rapport when he speaks to us.

The community's midwife commands instant rapport. We listen to her and her views about the world. There is no reason to expect she harbors some sinister agenda behind her statements.

What if we live in a metro area? Let's ask ourselves: who do we trust and believe?

The restaurant reviewer who tells us which restaurants have the best version of our favorite food.

The security guard at our apartment building who gives us the latest gossip.

Our exercise and walking partner who tells us the healthiest food to eat.

So why do these people have rapport with us? Obviously, their track record helps. Over time we've learned to trust and believe what they say.

But what if we don't have a track record?

What if we meet new people? What can we do to enhance our chances of creating rapport?

Even with strangers, we want them to trust and believe what we say.

Here are some shortcuts that will help us quickly create rapport with others.

#1: Smile.

When we smile, people want to believe and trust what we say. This is a hard-wired program that we get almost from birth.

A small baby lies in the crib. At only six weeks old, the baby cannot roll over, talk, or process this brand-new world. An adult leans over the crib and looks at the baby. To get the baby's trust, what does the adult do?

Smile.

And how does the baby react? With a smile.

Somehow, from only six weeks old, babies realize that a smile means friendship, and they are safe. This adult does not have sinister intentions.

So when we smile, people naturally want to believe and trust what we say.

Now is this program always accurate? Of course not!

Politicians smile. Bad-intentioned con men smile. Yet no one questions this program.

If someone smiles, it does not mean what they say can be believed or trusted. However, as humans, we take shortcuts. And our programmed shortcut is, "If someone smiles, that person can be trusted."

Ridiculous? Yes.

True? Yes.

So, if we want rapport with another person, smiling helps.

But what if we are not a person that always smiles?

Time to learn. If we are going to meet new individuals with a serious face, we handicap our chances to create rapport. Smiling isn't that difficult anyway. It takes 13 muscles on the left side of our face, 13 muscles on the right side of our face, maybe show a little bit of teeth, and try to be sincere.

Try it. It works.

But what if we talk facts with an accountant? Still works. What if we talk hard-core science with an engineer? Still works. Our chances of successful rapport increase every time we smile. Humans react predictably to smiles.

If our smile is sincere, others can tell. If our smile is insincere, others can tell that also. Humans read body language and facial expressions. If our intentions are sincere, they will show through in our smile. Sincere smiles work.

#2. Tell others facts they already believe.

When we tell others facts they already believe, this means we are smart, just like they are. They think we are fellow geniuses with great insights into the world.

Everyone has a point of view. When we agree with their point of view, they think, "Hey, you think like me. As a fellow genius, you see the world from the same perspective. Because we see the facts from the same perspective, we will make the same conclusions. So, whatever you say will perfectly align with my beliefs. I can trust and believe what you say next."

If we start our conversations with people by pointing out our differences, we lose. This set up walls of disbelief and skepticism. Now these people will critically censor our conversation. We will never achieve rapport, much less influence, if we start on the wrong foot.

For example, how will a stranger react if we start our conversation with criticism or pointing out their mistakes?

The stranger will think, "Whoa. You are wrong already. I don't make mistakes. And how dare you criticize what I did. You don't know the circumstances. You don't know me. You are an ... idiot. And I am sure you are wrong about everything else too!"

With strangers, we should definitely begin our conversations with something they agree with.

Imagine this: We stand on a street corner on a hot summer day. A stranger is near us, also waiting to cross the street. To start a conversation with rapport, what would we say? We might start by saying, "Pretty hot today." With sweat rolling down their forehead, the stranger might reply, "Yes, sure is hot today." We start with this common-knowledge fact naturally.

The opposite of creating rapport? If we wanted to start a conversation with this stranger and **not** create rapport, we could start by saying, "The Democrats sure are a lot smarter than the Republicans." Whoops!

Now we only have a 50% chance of rapport with this individual. If this individual is a Democrat supporter, yes, we have rapport. But if this individual is a Republican supporter, our credibility, our rapport, and our future influence are gone.

Common sense tells us to start conversations with agreement to establish rapport. We know this naturally. But before we talk to strangers, it is good practice to remember this rule. Early agreement helps create rapport.

People feel a bond when they have common elements of experience. We tend to like people who are more like us, and distrust people who are less like us.

Imagine we are from the United States, and decide to go to India.

Over a billion people are around us in India, and we meet a person from the United States. Instantly we feel rapport because we have something in common. Our conversation might go like this. "Where are you from?" The stranger replies, "I am from Florida." We reply by saying, "I am from California. We are neighbors!"

When everyone around us is different, we stretch to find commonalities. We feel better when we have common bonds with others.

Here are some examples of what we could say to build rapport early in our conversations.

- "I see you like cats also."

- "Looks like the business climate in our area is heading into a recession."

- "I love this team. How long have you been a fan?"

- "That was pretty spectacular!"

- "This tastes great."

- "You are probably wondering, how long will this take?"

- "We want more money in our lives."

- "It is hard to find true love at this nightclub."

- "Weekends are made for parties!"

- "Mondays are the worst day of the week."

- "We deserve more holidays in our lives."

- "I feel hungry also. Where should we eat?"

- "We need this, but we have to stay within budget."

- "This project is important, but we need more time."

- "It is fun to watch our children play."

It is not hard to find facts that we can agree upon with strangers.

If we need more examples, we could listen to campaign speeches. Politicians create rapport with their supporters by stating facts their supporters believe. The politician might say:

"We want lower taxes. And we want to uphold our country's values. Let's bring integrity to the government now."

And the supporters shout, "Yes! And here are our campaign donations."

Creating rapport with others is within our control.

But we are just starting. Let's make our rapport even better.

Deeper rapport.

Is rapport necessary to have influence over others?

Yes. There could be rare exceptions. But why risk ruining our chances for influence?

When we have rapport as our base, it is easy to take the next step up to influence. So, let's look at more ways to create rapport with the people we will want to influence.

#3. A fact, and another fact, and then our new idea.

When we tell people two facts in a row, their brains want to accept future statements from us as true, without judgment.

Human brains are underpowered. We can consciously judge only one thing at a time. That's all!

When we tell people a fact, they think, "Yes, I believe that fact to be true." And when we tell them another fact, they think, "Yes, I believe that fact to be true also. That is two facts in a row, and both are true. You are a trusted source. I don't need to judge what you say any more. Let me put my limited brainpower somewhere else in my life. I can accept what you say as true in the future."

After two true facts, we almost put people into a deep hypnotic trance. They want to accept what we say next as true, as long as it is reasonable. As humans, we constantly rely on shortcuts to survive. We can't maintain critical thinking for every input into our brains. We have to be selective. Millions of bits of information bombard our brains every second. Consciously, we can only pay attention to one thing at a time.

Let's do an example of using two true facts, and then introducing our new idea that we want people to believe.

"Not a cloud in the sky. A beautiful day. I think we will enjoy this day." Two facts, and then we predict that we will enjoy this day. The people we tell this to will want to accept "We will enjoy this day," as true. Pretty simple.

If we wanted to get a new, reasonable statement inside people's brains, we would state two facts in a row. And then, we would introduce the new statement. Let's do some examples.

"The appetizer was excellent. And this entrée is delicious. I bet the dessert will be amazing!"

"Your business needs this tool. But you have to stay within budget. This tool will easily fit into your current budget for the year."

"Our children deserve a better education. And, the results from other schools prove this reading program works. It makes sense for us to adopt it immediately."

"The weekend is coming. We want to have fun. This canoe race looks like a great activity for us." (Yeah, I fell for this. But thinking back, I did have a lot of fun and the memories will last forever.)

"Our boss is a jerk. He never listens to us. We should start our own business and be our own boss."

"Things are expensive now. Our salary doesn't go far enough. We should look at ways to earn more money for our families."

"At age 40, our skin begins to wrinkle. And, our face is our best first impression. Let's try something new to hold back the aging of our skin."

"We are proud of our country. We want to uphold our country's values. Elect me so I can help you keep these values in place." (This sounds like every politician's speech.)

"The weekend is coming. You will want permission to go out with your friends. I think now would be a good time to clean your room."

"Our lives are hard. We are in a rut. Let's look at more options for our lives."

"We agree this program doesn't work. We need to make more progress or we won't be re-elected. Let's try this new option to see if it helps."

After two facts, our suggestions of new information feel easy for people to accept. By agreeing first, we can stay in rapport.

With rapport, we can transfer new ideas to others. If we fall out of rapport, people will block our new ideas. Before pushing new ideas into people's minds, let's work on creating rapport first. This increases our chances of success.

#4. "Well, you know how …"

This is a verbal command to the subconscious mind. The phrase, "Well, you know how …" is so common that people don't even hear us say these words. When we want people to believe what we say next, we naturally start with the phrase, "Well, you know how …"

Listen to this conversation by the coffee machine at work.

First person: "Well, you know how the traffic is so bad coming in on the freeway every day?"

Second person: "Well, you know how we waste two hours every day commuting back and forth?"

Third person: "Well, you know how this job interferes with our week? We could do a lot if we didn't have to commute an extra two hours five times a week."

Fourth person: "Well, you know how our football team let us down again this Sunday?"

As we can see, if someone wants the rest of the group to agree, they naturally say the words, "Well, you know how ..."

We hear these words so often that we don't notice the phrase. But when we say these words, here is what happens in the minds of the listeners.

They think, "Well, if I already know how, then whatever you say next must be true. Because what I already know is true. No further proof needed. No testimonials, no fact sheets, because I already know that what I know is true."

So we start with the phrase, "Well, you know how ..." Then, if our next fact seems semi-reasonable, most people accept what we say as true. Again, this is a shortcut our minds use. We can't stop everything in our lives to question every bit of information that enters our brain.

Here are some examples of using this phrase:

"Well, you know how we desperately want our children to get the best education possible?"

"Well, you know how you want the keys to the car this weekend?"

"Well, you know how your salespeople are struggling because they don't have enough leads?"

"Well, you know how our paychecks don't go far enough?"

"Well, you know how everyone secretly dreams of being rich?"

"Well, you know how we want this result, but we just don't know how to get there?"

"Well, you know how health doesn't come from an antibiotic capsule?"

"Well, you know how hard it is to lose weight?"

"Well, you know how our country's values changed with the current political climate?"

Creating rapport with people is beginning to look pretty easy. With simple verbal commands, we can convince their minds to accept what we say as true.

This is fun. Let's look at some more verbal commands.

#5. "Most people."

When we say, "Most people," what do other people think?

They think, "I want to fit in. I want to be safe. I want to be like most people. Then if I make a decision, and the decision does not work out, I won't be criticized. But if I do something unique, something different, and it doesn't work out, I will open myself to ridicule from my peers."

Yes, it is natural for us to want to fit in. Think of every teenager in high school. One of the highest-priority programs in their minds is to fit in with the group.

How did we get this program? The program is called "survival." This is a high priority for all of us. We feel safer in numbers.

We walk through a dark alley at night. Do we want to walk through alone, or with a group of other people?

We hear about a new medicine. Do we want to be the first person to take that medicine?

There are two restaurants. One is full, the other is empty. Which restaurant feels safer for us to visit?

We watch the construction of a new bungee jump. Do we want to be the first person to test it?

There is a minefield ahead. Do we want to be the first person to cross that minefield?

Do you see the pattern? We feel safer with our decisions if other people think the same. We want to see other people go before us and survive.

When we talk to people, by starting with the words, "Most people," we make it easier for them to agree. Rapport is getting other people to believe us and trust us. If we can't build rapport, we will never get to influence.

Here are examples of "Most people" statements.

"Most people think this tastes delicious. Want to try?"

"Most business people want profits, so they pay close attention to their bottom-line budget."

"Most parents want their children to get a better education than they did."

"Most people look forward to coffee breaks."

"Most people want a corruption-free government. Elect me to lead the way."

"Most teachers can't wait for school holidays."

"Most people like paying less for things. Let me show you how to save money on this."

"Most neighbors want to support the local high school band."

"Most buyers are willing to set aside a few minutes, if it means big savings for their company."

"Most people" is an easy phrase to say. People react with smiles. Everyone uses these words naturally. When we say the words, "Most people," people make an instant decision to be part of the most people group.

#6. More command words.

Many word phrases command others to believe and trust what we say. Here are a few more.

"Everybody knows."

"Everybody says."

"Most people agree."

When we start to notice these word sequences, we can add more to our list. Let's do a few examples of using these three-word sequences.

"Everybody knows it is hard to get a raise here."

"Everybody knows our school budget isn't big enough for this project."

"Everybody knows that your school grades will be important when you apply for scholarships."

"Everybody says the economy's in trouble."

"Everybody says we don't want to repeat our past mistakes."

"Everybody says we want better control of our government's finances."

"Most people agree that jobs interfere with our week."

"Most people agree that diets never work in the long run."

It is easier to have conversations with people when we start with their agreement. When people trust us and believe us, we can move ideas from our heads to their heads.

Let's try to put a few of these rapport skills together. In this example, imagine we are selling a diet product to a customer at our store. See if we can pick up the rapport skills used.

"Losing weight is difficult. And most people don't have time to do hours of exercise. And well, you know how losing weight was difficult in the past? Everybody knows there must be a better way. Let me show you the solution to weight loss that everyone is talking about."

Our potential customer anxiously awaits the introduction to the product he or she will be purchasing shortly.

Another example?

Imagine we wanted to convince our neighbors to put exercise and play equipment in the empty land near our homes. We could say, "Give me money. I want to build a park for the kids." Direct, but not effective. Let's try using a few rapport skills.

"Everyone knows our neighborhood children have to play somewhere. And well, you know how they are currently playing in our streets? Most people here worry about our children's safety. Plus, we get that occasional damage to some of our parked cars. Let's create a little park in this vacant land so our children can play there safely. Plus, we won't have to worry about broken windows and car damage any longer."

This is getting to be fun. We talk, people nod in agreement. That is a great feeling when people hear our message.

Word commands are great to get people to agree with us, but let's look at something even more powerful.

OTHER WAYS TO CREATE RAPPORT.

To get deeper rapport and understanding from others, here are three more skills.

#7. Listen.

Rapport is easier if people like us. Who do people like more? People who talk, or people who listen? The answer is obvious.

Every person wants to be heard. If we listen, people will feel that we are the most amazing conversationalist in the history of mankind. They go home and tell their spouse, "I had the most amazing conversation. I talked. The other person listened. The other person was the greatest conversationalist I have ever met."

Of course this is an exaggeration, but this is how people feel.

Think about others. Their bosses don't listen to them. Their coworkers don't listen to them. Their families don't listen to them. If we take the time to listen, we will build rapport. People will like us and will want to believe what we say. We like agreeing with our friends.

How hard is it to listen?

If we are an introvert, it is easy. We just stand there. Plus, we may have a natural interest in what other people say.

If we are an extrovert, this is hard. We have to bite our tongue until it bleeds. We are so excited about what we have to say, we rarely make the other person feel special by pausing and listening to what they say.

Extroverts have a problem with rapport. Listeners feel like they are being "talked to" instead of having a conversation. When the extroverts dominate the conversation, the listeners may seem polite. But they secretly wish they could participate in the conversation. This is not a good formula for building strong rapport.

For instance, we go to buy something. The salesman talks and talks, never allowing us a chance to comment or ask questions. What are our feelings? Stress, resentment, frustration.

We must allow others to talk.

So, if we are a natural extrovert, how do we train our minds to be attentive when others speak?

First, we have to release our current agenda. We want to tell other people what to think, how to think, when to think, and what to do about it.

Second, we should stop talking, and attempt to get feedback from others. We want them to feel like they are part of our conversation.

Third, we should create an intense interest in learning from what others say. If they are more knowledgeable in a certain topic, we can make mental notes to increase our own knowledge. If we possess more expertise on the subject, we can learn what others are feeling as they are on their learning journey. This will help us communicate with them later.

Listening is hard. There are courses on improving our listening skills. But if we make an honest attempt to be interested in what the other people say, we will create better rapport.

#8. Point out a flaw or imperfection in what we suggest.

People don't expect perfect solutions to every problem. When we make proposals, others start making judgments. They start thinking about the good parts **and** the bad parts. Why? Because they have survival programs too. They want to be sure that our proposals won't harm them or make things worse.

But when we point out a weakness in our proposal, they think, "You are a fair person. You are not trying to sell us your agenda. Instead, you point out the strong points and the weak points. I don't have to question if you have an ulterior motive to manipulate me. You even help me notice the weaknesses."

When people perceive us as fair, they trust and believe our ideas. They want to take our ideas into their minds without adding harsh judgment and skepticism.

Every suggestion or idea we propose has flaws. Nothing is 100% perfect in the real world. If we point out a minor flaw, that helps our listeners accept the main part of our proposal. We have trust and rapport.

Want some examples?

Example #1. "The reduced carbohydrate diet is one of the fastest ways to lose weight. The downside is that you will crave French fries and pasta for the first 72 hours."

Example #2. "This insurance will protect our high school team when they play extreme sports. But since we only have this much money left in our budget, we will have to give up having a logo on our team bus."

Example #3. "Starting your own business is exciting. But you will miss your relationships and daily chats at the coffee machine at work."

Example #4. "This car accelerates faster than any other car in its class. However, you will hurt your average fuel efficiency if you drive like a racecar driver."

Example #5. "This do-it-yourself kit will save us a lot of money. Are we willing to do the construction work ourselves?"

Example #6. "Come to my house for drinks and a barbecue on Saturday. You will miss washing your car and mowing your lawn, but you could do that on a different day."

People like having conversations with people who are fair. When we show that we look at the good parts **and** the bad parts, people feel comfortable with us.

#9. Body language and micro-facial expressions.

A stranger walks in the door. We take a quick look at the stranger to determine if the stranger will be a friend or a threat. Again, our survival program is at work.

How quickly do we judge this person? Almost immediately. It is not fair, but this is what humans do to survive. One bad mistake, and it is over. So, we are very cautious whenever we meet someone new.

How do we judge this person so quickly, even before this person says his first words?

We read their body language, and we read their micro-facial expressions. Micro-facial expressions happen too quickly for our conscious minds to make judgment. Humans can create almost 30 micro-facial expressions in a second! A few people can read faces consciously, but they are very specialized in this area. For most of us, we just get a feeling from our subconscious minds about this person.

Our subconscious minds keep a database of thousands of people's faces. Our subconscious minds reference other strangers' faces from our past. It looks for clues of what their intentions could be. A person does not have to show up with a hockey mask and an axe for us to make a judgment about their intentions. If someone has bad intentions for us, our subconscious minds can read that in their face.

Our pets have this micro-facial reading ability also. They say dogs can remember every move and expression of their owners. While I don't know if this is 100% true, or even how researchers could measure it, there is some truth to this.

Imagine one morning, we walk into the living room and say to our pets, "Let's hop into the car for a fun ride!"

Our pets take one look at us and immediately hide underneath the sofa. Why? They know we are taking them to the vet.

How did they know that today was the day we would take them to the vet? Did they take their little paws and break into our diary? No. They read our micro-facial expressions. They remembered the last time we said the words, "Let's hop into the car for a fun ride!" They remember the expression on our face. On that day they ended up at the vet's office, with needles in their hindquarters.

Pets know. So do humans. We read other people's faces all the time, looking for clues to their intentions.

What about our personal body language and micro-facial expressions? The people we meet judge us based upon our body language and micro-facial expressions also.

Ouch! How do we control our body language and up to 30 micro-facial expressions per second? Do we need to take a long, complicated course on how to twist our faces? Of course not.

Our body language and our micro-facial expressions reflect our internal intentions. If we change our intentions, it will show. Try this little experiment.

Suppose we are a sales representative. Right before we to talk to our potential client, we stand in front of a mirror. We say to ourselves, "I am going to crush this person like a grape! I will force this person to accept my agenda no matter how much he resists."

If we walk into the potential client's office with this intention in our minds, the potential client will resist us and our suggestions. He might not know why he resists, but he will be skeptical and resist what we offer.

Now, imagine we did this instead. Right before we step inside the door to talk to our potential client, we stand in front of the mirror again. This time we say to ourselves, "This potential client has a problem. I will offer this potential client one more option for solving his problem. He can then decide if our option will serve him or not."

When we walk through the door with this intention in our minds, our body language and micro-facial expressions adjust. The potential client will feel better about accepting our proposal.

Yes, people can read our intentions. Let's make sure our intentions show on our faces and in our body language before we make our proposal.

What about John Doe?

If John Doe took the time to learn these rapport skills, at least his audience would trust and believe what he said.

Now John would have a solid rapport platform. He could then start building influence with this foundation of belief and trust.

The next step: Influence.

That's enough background on these basic common sense skills on creating rapport. Rapport is great, but it is not enough to create influence with others.

Remember, rapport means, "We can trust you and believe what you say."

But influence could mean, "I trust and believe what you say. I respect you. I respect your judgment. I want to take action on what you suggest."

Let's see which actions John Doe can take to start creating influence with his coworkers, friends, family, and even with strangers.

STRATEGIES FOR CREATING INFLUENCE WITH OTHERS.

Now that we have rapport with our audience, we will start to create influence.

Influence is easier when people agree with us. If people disagree with us, we will invest more time creating rapport. Then, our next step will be to influence them.

And like rapport, we want to have many different strategies to create influence. Some of these strategies will be easy and within our comfort zone. Other strategies may not be useful in a particular situation.

But with a full toolbox of options, we can pick the right strategy to get the influence we need.

Let's start with some easy strategies of how our mythical John Doe could create influence in his office.

CREATING INFLUENCE:
STRATEGY #1.

Become the organizer.

A major charity in the United States uses this fundraising marketing strategy. Once a year, they get one person in every office to go desk-to-desk, soliciting pledges for donations. Most people in the office pledge a small amount of money to be taken out of their paycheck every month. This one person is in charge of giving the coworkers forms that authorize the charity deduction.

This is a yearly ritual. The charity says, "Give your money to us, and we will distribute your money to the appropriate charities. Then, you don't have to listen to charity requests all year long. Pledge now to give money to our big charity. We will take care of the rest."

John Doe volunteers for this job. He wasn't elected. No one authorized him to go desk-to-desk and collect pledges. He just volunteered. And, since no one else wanted to volunteer for this job, John had no competition.

Now, what happens to the relationship between John and each individual coworker?

First, the coworker actually notices John for the very first time. Second, in each coworker's minds, there is a small seed planted that John is important. He is in charge of the office's charity drive for the year. The coworkers subconsciously assign some power to

John. With this power comes respect. And with respect comes ... influence.

Did John create massive influence from this one fundraising campaign? No, but he made progress. John now has some importance and imagined authority in his coworkers' minds.

One way to establish influence with others is to become the organizer or leader of a project or trip.

In this example, John made a smart choice. As the appointed collector of pledges, his job was easy. No selling. No convincing. The employees expected someone to put the annual charity request form on their desks.

John risked nothing to get this influence. He borrowed the influence and the associated power from the charity. Plus, the management at the office expected everyone to pledge and donate something. The social pressure to donate made John's job easy. All John had to do was say, "Here is your form. Fill out how much you would like to donate every month from your paycheck. I will pick up the form a little bit later."

If we need influence, we should take the time to look around us to see what we can organize.

Let's start with trips. When a group goes on a trip, it feels like herding cats. Frustrating, for sure. Because organizing is an unpaid task, few people will volunteer to take charge of a trip's organization. What kind of trips could we organize?

If we worked in a branch office, and the entire branch office had to go to the main office, someone must organize the bus. Someone has to let everyone know what time the bus leaves. And of course, someone has to let everyone know what time the bus returns. The person who organizes appears to be in charge, even though no one actually gave that person power.

We could organize a trip where several families holiday together. Or a trip for several people to a sports event or concert.

What about a holiday gift exchange? Someone has to get a hat, and then cut slips of paper with everyone's name. Then, they'll need to arrange for people to each draw out a name to determine who they will be giving a gift to during the holiday.

Could we organize the annual holiday party at work? Easy. We don't have to beg people to come to a party. They love parties. Our role might be to find a location and set the date.

The organizer assumes the position of power, and with that power comes influence.

Remember the organizer of my canoe adventure of horror?

All he did was come up with the idea and announce the idea at our office. No one else had any ideas for the weekend. We all chimed in, "That sounds like a great suggestion." We willingly gave power and influence to the organizer.

Many people are not creative. They go along in life doing the bare minimum. With a little creative thought, we can find or create many opportunities to be the organizer.

Here are some more organizer opportunity ideas:

- A book club.
- A community clean-up day.
- Getting volunteers for election day.
- A holiday dinner for the homeless shelter.

- The annual neighborhood street hockey event of parents versus children.

People will remember us as the organizer. That gives us influence with them. Not only will they pay attention when we speak, but they are more willing to take action on our suggestions.

CREATING INFLUENCE: STRATEGY #2.

We can deposit emotional units of goodwill.

When we network with people, they mentally keep a ledger of our relationship. This ledger shows them how much we helped them, versus how much they helped us. If we are a taker, our power is diminished. If we are a giver, they feel that imbalance in their emotional bank account, and will want to even that ledger. They feel obligated to at least listen to our ideas and opinions.

Here is an example of these emotional units of deposit.

Imagine our daughter was in a burning building. Someone rescues our daughter. Instantly we create a huge debt in our emotional bank account balance with the person who saved our daughter's life.

Of course, small favors are not that dramatic. Most people notice small favors, and these favors add up. Here are some examples of favors that create balances in emotional bank accounts.

- Picking someone up when their car breaks down.
- Giving advice on an inexpensive family weekend activity.
- Listening to someone's story of grief.
- Letting others know when there is a special sale at their favorite store.
- Bringing a meal to someone's house when they are ill.
- Patiently listening to someone's boring stories.

- Helping someone solve their computer problem.
- Telling someone when there is a movie or show that they would enjoy.
- Watching someone's children when they couldn't get a babysitter.
- Having lunch together, and buying their lunch.
- Supporting their opinions in group conversations.
- Refraining from judging their mistakes or pointing out their failures.
- Helping them find the right person to network with.
- Giving someone a great lead on a potential job opening.

As we can see, any time we do someone a favor or provide some help, that action deposits emotional units. This helps us with our influence.

Creating influence:
Strategy #3.

Public speaking. Oh my!

Most people prefer dental surgery, moldy holiday fruit cake, and torture rather than speaking in public. This is nightmare material.

We fear standing in front of a group and being judged. We fear forgetting what to say, then blushing with embarrassment.

Because of these hard-core fears, we naturally respect anyone who speaks in public. We mentally see public speakers as people with intelligence, influence, and leadership qualities. Why? Because they spoke in public.

These qualities may not be deserved, but we assign them to the speakers anyway. As long as we don't have to speak in public, we are content to sit in our chairs and be influenced by the speakers. We allow speakers to guide our thoughts and sometimes our actions. Public speakers claim a powerful position in our minds.

They're in charge. They talk, we listen. They direct the group's thinking. We tend to go along with the suggestions, and along with the crowd.

Who is the only person standing? Well, that person must be the expert. And of course, that means that person has power and influence.

Now, who **should** be standing in front of the group? That person should be us!

But if the thought of public speaking traumatizes us, what should we do?

If we want to increase our influence, then we must overcome this irrational fear. And oh, that is so easy to say, but much harder to do!

So let's attack our fear of public speaking now. Others mastered their public speaking fear, and we can too. Let's learn what we can do to destroy this fear. Here are some general guidelines:

1. Know more than our audience. It we stand in front of a kindergarten class to speak about reading, no problem. We don't feel embarrassed or intimidated by the five-year-old children. They could try to harass us, but our superior knowledge wins. Plus, their teacher could frown and put them in their place.

In this example, we know more than our audience. When we become an expert on our topic, our fear fades away. That's a good reason to be a micro-expert in a narrow niche of information. Then we will always be the most knowledgeable person in the room. More about becoming a micro-expert later.

Want to visualize the opposite? If we choose a brand-new topic and our audience knows more than we do, expect a brutal experience. Decency standards prevent us from describing what will happen.

No speaker ever wants an audience that knows more about the topic, or has a unique angle on the topic. Be an expert on a narrow, narrow niche, and we will feel confident when we speak.

Prepare. Prepare. Prepare. And then we can relax when we speak to less-informed people.

2. Practice. First, by ourselves. Every word phrase becomes a tongue-twister the first time. Don't worry. The next time, the word phrases get easier. The first time is the hardest. We build a bit of muscle memory on how to say things with a quick practice or two.

Next, we practice in front of live people.

Want to take creating influence seriously? Enrolling in Toastmasters or a Dale Carnegie public speaking course is an excellent idea. Both organizations help us overcome our fear. How? Because we speak in front of our classmates regularly. Don't worry, they start small. We only speak a few words in our first class.

Is this investment worth our time?

Absolutely. Think about how many times we handicap ourselves with our fear to stand up and speak. When this fear goes away, a huge weight leaves our shoulders.

Now we can voice our opinions. The people around us say nothing. Their fear of public speaking silences their voices. And they award us power and influence.

Where can we find more opportunities to speak in public? Let's make a list.

1. At our school's parent-teacher day.

2. At our daughter's award banquet.

3. We can volunteer to be the emcee at our cousin's wedding.

4. At the local Commerce luncheons. We also get a free meal from them for speaking for 15 minutes about our particular expertise.

5. We can present travel options at our monthly association or club.

6. We can present our ideas to the homeowners' association for reducing common expenses.

7. Offer to be the spokesman or spokeswoman for a local charity. They always look for someone to present their charity to groups who can put their charity in the best possible light.

8. Offer to teach a class at the adult education night school.

9. Offer to teach a craft at the local community center.

10. Be the first audience member to take the microphone when a speaker asks for questions from the audience.

11. Volunteer to read the new regulations and rules for the office.

12. Read the meeting notes or reports at the next meeting.

There are many opportunities for us to speak. All we have to do is volunteer.

But I need to overcome that fear quickly!

We need a shortcut now. Waiting for a class to start will take too long. How can we conquer our fear of public speaking in the next ten minutes?

Let's figure this out.

Here are the two biggest fears of public speaking:

1. We worry we will forget what to say next. Then, we will stand in the front of the room with our mouth open and our face blushing. Every second will feel like an eternity.

2. We worry how others will judge us. Will they be bored? Will they walk out while we are talking? Will they think we are ignorant? What if they don't pay attention?

These are real fears. However, we can solve both fears quickly. How?

By telling a story.

This shortcut makes us an interesting and effective public speaker immediately.

Let's see how telling a story solves these two big fears.

Suppose someone asked us how we arrived at the office today. Could we answer? Of course. We know how we came to the office.

We would say, "I got into my car, backed out of my driveway, and pulled onto Fifth Street. As soon as I came to Highway 109, I turned left to come into the city. Apparently I wanted to get to the office a little too quickly, so the local police officer stopped me and interviewed me. Then, I received a ticket as a reminder to stay within the speed limit in the future. Well, I continued on Highway 109, until I turned on to Mall Avenue. I pulled into the parking lot. Locked my car. Took the elevator up to our office, and that is how I got to work today."

Why we can remember every step of the story? Because it is a story. Human minds are wired for stories. We love stories. Our minds think in stories. This gets better, but we'll cover this more later.

We can study for a history exam, but 15 minutes later we can't remember the dates. We struggle to remember facts.

But stories? We can tell you what happened in a movie we saw three years ago. Our minds recall stories and remember the details.

So if we must speak, let's tell a story. We will never worry about remembering what comes next.

Now, Fear #1 is gone.

But what about Fear #2?

What if we are afraid of how others judge us when we speak?

The answer is: stories.

Our audiences consist of people. People have addictions to stories. That is why they like books. That is why they like movies. That is why they love reading Hollywood gossip. Stories feel like a sugar rush to our minds.

When children are two years old, as soon as they can form a sentence, they say, "Mommy, Daddy, please tell me a story." They love stories.

Our stories create movies in the minds of others. They feel as if they are in our stories. If we walk by three people, and one person is telling a story, what would our minds tell us to do? Our minds would say, "Stop. You must listen to that story."

Stories grab our attention. We want to know what happens next. Stories help satisfy the big program in our minds, survival.

Stories instruct us on how to survive in the future when we have a similar experience.

So, we sit around the campfire and tell stories. Someone says, "When you see a big cat with these extra-long teeth, stay away. They want to eat you."

Stories give us predictive behavior. In the future, if we are out on a hike and we see a huge cat with big teeth, our survival program says, "Even though you've never seen one of these before, they are dangerous. Remember that story from the campfire? Don't go near that cat."

There are so many reasons humans feel drawn to stories. It has to be a really, really terrible story to keep someone from listening intently.

When we tell a story, people mentally sit on the edge of their seats. They want to know what happens next.

Looks like we've solved the second fear.

Other people love our stories. They won't walk out. They want to know how our story ends.

Our fears of public speaking? Gone.

The short story is: we can solve our fears by telling a story.

How much influence will public speaking give us?

More than we expect. Much more. Plus, our confidence grows.

Few people want to speak in front of a group. Few people will challenge the ideas put forth by someone with influence. And who is that person with influence? That would be us. We took the initiative to stand and speak.

Need a quick way to solve public speaking fears?

Read the book, *Public Speaking Magic: Success and Confidence in the First 20 Seconds.*

Why? Because we learn that all the judging by our audience is over in the first 20 seconds. The great news is that we only have to be good for the first 20 seconds!

If we are a beginner, no problem. Anyone can learn to manage their first 20 seconds.

Once our audience decides to like us, everything else is easier.

CREATING INFLUENCE: STRATEGY #4.

Use stories.

At family gatherings, I enjoy messing with my grandchildren, nieces, and nephews. Like all children, they love to hear stories. They can't wait. They beg me to tell them stories.

I start the story with believable facts. Mention people they know. Things they are familiar with.

Then slowly I stretch the facts to something unbelievable. But they continue to believe the unbelievable, because the story started with hardcore facts.

When they go back and tell their parents the stories I told, their parents roll their eyes. They tell their children, "Never believe him again!" But the next time I see them, history repeats. The human brain has flaws.

People love stories. Stories help us get our message inside of their heads. If we can weave our intentions and facts into stories, it is easier for others to accept our message.

Let's look at our minds. To protect ourselves, we have natural defenses. When a stranger talks to us, our minds automatically throw up these barriers:

- Be careful. Don't believe what strangers say.

- Be skeptical. Strangers have agendas.

- Be negative. Protect ourselves from new ideas and information that may not be true.

- Activate the "too-good-to-be-true" filter.

- Ask ourselves, "So what is the catch?"

Yes, when strangers talk to us, their words bounce off our foreheads and trickle to the floor. We resist new things that strangers tell us.

But stories bypass these defenses.

When we hear a story, our minds react, "Story? Oh yes!" We are like puppies waiting for a treat. Our minds crave stories.

This is an easy way to influence the knowledge and opinions of others. We simply wrap our message with a story.

To help our audience, we can signal that we are about to tell a story. Here are some openings we can use:

- "Once upon a time."

This shouts, "A story is coming!" But, it does more. It brings back good feelings from our childhood. Why not put our audience in a good mood?

- "When I was young."

People want to know what happened to us when we were young. It must be important if we are telling them now.

- "Can I tell you a secret?"

Curiosity always wins. This is one of the strongest programs in the human mind. How can anyone resist listening to what we are about to share with them?

- "Let me tell you what happened to me."

People are polite. They will give us permission to tell them our story.

There are many more wonderful openings, but we get the idea. We will:

1. Signal to others that we will tell a story.

2. Watch their eyes light up.

3. Tell our message wrapped in a story.

4. Watch how our story influences our listeners.

Are these the only types of stories?

Of course not. There are many types of stories we could tell. For example, there are "before and after" transformation stories. Testimonials are a great example of this technique. Here is how it might sound.

"Let me tell you what happened to my daughter. I didn't believe she could ever read at her grade level. No matter how hard she tried, she couldn't keep up. After three sessions with 'Tutor by Us,' her reading level jumped three grades. That is why we recommend them to all parents who have children who struggle to read."

Our message is now in our listeners' heads. Stories make it easy.

We don't have to be a professional story-teller, so don't worry. Most of us tell stories with ease. We've told stories all of our lives.

Want an excellent how-to book full of great story openings? Get the book, *Storytelling Secrets for Successful Speeches: 7 strategies for telling stories people love,* by Mark Davis. Just pick from hundreds of easy openers. It's a quick and pleasant read.

Do we want our stories to be more interesting?

Our stories should have a bit of drama or tension. Here is the basic outline of a story:

1. There was a problem.

2. Then here is what happened.

3. And now, here is the current situation.

Not too complicated, right? But did we notice the story started with the problem? Isn't that how many of our favorite movies start, with the problem? If there is no tension or drama, if there are no problems, the story would be boring.

Would we have interest in a story like this?

"A mother loves her children. She loves them every day. She will continue to love them in the future."

This story wouldn't make the news. It wouldn't be the story on the front page of our national newspaper.

Now, the story would be more interesting if it went like this.

"A mother loves her children. When she wakes up in the morning, her children have vanished. And the only clue she has is a cracker-addicted, difficult-to-understand parrot who has a lisp."

This might not be the plot of a best-selling novel, but we get the idea. Our story should have a problem from the beginning.

Salespeople forget this.

When most salespeople talk to prospects, they want to give long presentations. They go on and on about the features and benefits of the company's products. They talk about their company background and awards.

What do prospects think? Boring!

Maybe this is one reason why we dislike salespeople. Of course, movies and television routinely put salespeople in a bad light, so that increases our skepticism too.

Do we now see why salespeople have difficulty creating strong influence with their prospects?

What should salespeople talk about?

About their prospects. What is the most interesting subject to prospects? Themselves. Yes, prospects are selfish just like everyone else. We are the most important people in our lives.

We have to sell our ideas to others.

If we need to sell our audience on our message, talk about the audience. At least they will enjoy our subject matter.

But can we be even more effective? Yes. By talking about the problems in our audiences' lives. Everyone thinks about themselves all day long. We worry about our problems. When we talk about the problems in the lives of our audience, we have their undivided attention.

Next, we tell a story about how we solved similar problems for others. Our audience desperately hangs on our every word. They want to listen.

Look at this sales presentation from a roofing salesman. He tells a story. We listen. The salesman says:

"Last week's storm was terrible. Every roof in the city suffered damage. I know you worry that if it rains again, all of your possessions are vulnerable to water damage. You want your roof to prevent water damage to your most valuable possessions. Here is what we did for some of your neighbors. We installed a temporary roof, and it only took a few hours. This temporary roof stops additional water damage. This protects your home until a permanent roof can be installed."

This was a simple story of events. He brought up the problem early in the story. This doesn't take much skill.

Let's do another story.

Imagine that we decide to run for political office. We have to influence voters to support us and take action. Our campaign speech could sound like this.

1. "We elected the anti-business party three years ago. They shut down the corrupt industries, the polluting industries, and the companies that only offered low wages. Then, we taxed 100% of the profits of the remaining companies to fund more programs. Unfortunately, since all the industries closed, we created massive unemployment." (There was a problem.)

2. "With no jobs, it became difficult for us to afford the payments on our homes and cars." (Then here is what happened.)

3. "So now we are in trouble, the banks are in trouble, and our local economy is a mess." (Here is the current situation.)

4. "So elect me and my running mates next month, so we can change the mistakes of the past." (We want them to take action and vote for us.)

No political viewpoint should be taken from this example. We only want to illustrate the speech structure politicians use to influence others to vote for them.

How about another story?

"Currently we rank 49th in education out of the 50 school districts in the state. This is a disgrace. We used to be in the top five, and consistently won awards of excellence. Our teachers felt well-paid and happy. We have cut our teacher salaries. We lost our best teachers to other schools. Now we have more teacher absenteeism. We pay extra for substitute teachers. Our school district saved nothing from this salary-cutting policy. For the exact same cost, we created a worse education system for our district."

Do stories like this sway people? Do we influence people with our stories? Yes.

Our best stories stick inside people's heads. They can't get our stories out of their minds. The stories agitate the thoughts in their brains until they finally want to take action.

So how do we wrap our facts and intentions in stories?

Here are more examples.

Fact version. "There are not enough parking spaces for our employees and visitors."

Story version. "Our best customer came to visit today. Because there was no place for him to park, he parked in our competitor's parking lot. He then visited our competitor. A few minutes ago, I received a cancellation on his last order."

Ouch! Someone is going to pay attention to this problem and take action.

Fact version. "I know I am in kindergarten, but I need a pair of $80 designer jeans."

Story version. "I know you told me to be brave on my first day of school. But all the children were wearing designer jeans except me. They made fun of me. I tried not to cry. But I'm so sorry, I cried. They wouldn't play with me. They told me to stand far away from them in the playground. No one would talk to me. I am so sorry, I tried to do my best to be brave."

Guess who is going shopping?

Yes, children are naturals at this.

Fact version. "This golf club is called the Pile Driver. It adds distance to your game."

Story version. "Imagine your boss is your partner in the four-some. Everyone hit their first drives a little over 200 yards to play it safe. Now it is your turn. Your boss looks at you and says, 'We have to beat these guys.' So you reach into your bag, pull out your

Pile Driver, tee up the ball. And whack! Your ball soars over 300 yards down the middle of the fairway. Your boss looks at you and says, "We have to talk about that vice president position when we get back to the office.'"

Guess who is buying a Pile Driver golf club today?

Exaggerated a little? Sure. But we felt intrigued by the story. And did the story present this Pile Driver golf club as something special? Yes.

Stories create great connections with people. We remember stories told around the campfire and over fancy coffee at the local coffee shop.

If we wrap our messages with a story, we can influence our audience's thoughts and actions.

CREATING INFLUENCE: STRATEGY #5.

Become a micro-expert.

People respect experts and follow their advice.

To become an expert in medicine, we could invest eight or ten years of our lives in advanced schooling. To become an expert on computer systems or engineering, it would take many years of study and experience.

But why choose such a big area of knowledge? Why not choose to be an expert in a tiny niche area? Anyone can become an expert by quickly searching for a few facts on the Internet.

The sheer amount of knowledge and information available to humans is huge! No one can focus on all the information. There is too much information for any one person to learn.

If we learned a lot about a very small topic, we would know more than 99.99% of everyone. That would make us a ... micro-expert.

How micro? Let's do an extreme example.

Imagine becoming an expert on the social habits of guinea pigs in high-altitude climates such as Ecuador. After reading one Internet article, we know more than everyone at our jobs. Read four or five articles, and we know more than almost everyone in our city.

Now, do we want to be an expert on the social habits of guinea pigs in high altitudes? I don't think so. But the point is there is so much knowledge, no one can be an expert in everything. People look for experts. They know they can't be experts or know everything. They would come to us for our expert knowledge on guinea pigs.

Imagine we sold diet products. It is hard to be a diet expert. People would expect us to have a medical degree, a PhD in science, or have years of experience as a researcher. But our strategy could be to become an expert in a very small niche of area of weight loss. Let's see what we could do.

1. We could become an expert on exercise.

However, there are already plenty of personal trainers and experts out there. Too much competition, and that means we would have to learn a lot to stand out. We need to make our niche smaller.

We decide that overweight people hate exercise. They hate going to the gym. They hate the ritual of dressing up in special exercise clothes to go on a walk and be target practice for the neighborhood's dogs. So, what do we do?

We become an expert on three or four exercises that overweight people find easy to do. Overweight people come to us and say, "I heard that you have some exercises that are easy to do." We could explain these exercises, because we have influence. We are the experts on these easy exercises. And, they would buy diet products from us. After all, we are the experts.

2. Imagine we are an energy consultant.

We recommend that families switch their electricity billing to our service. Most families refuse. They would only see a small amount of savings every month. For them, they don't think it is worth their time to change. So, we become an expert on using coupons to save money.

Community groups and social clubs might invite us to speak. We give the listeners great ways to use coupons and save money. Our audience is in the mindset of saving money. We are the coupon experts. And now it will be easy to influence them to switch their electricity billing. After all, we know more about coupons and saving money than most people.

3. As a local banker, we become the ultimate expert at mortgage reduction payments.

We even write short articles for the local newspaper. Everyone in the community knows, "If we want to save money on our mortgage payments, this is the person to see."

When people come into the bank and ask questions about their mortgage, they come to us, the expert at mortgage reduction. Since we are an expert, they automatically assume we are an expert in all areas of banking. They put their trust in us. We have the influence to guide them to better banking products.

4. The local sports club needs a new managing director.

Duties? To oversee the club's finances and to conduct the monthly meeting for club members. If we become an expert on

"Robert's Rules of Order" for conducting meetings, we gain the club members' respect. The meetings move smoothly. Because we are an expert in handling meetings, the members again assume that we would be good in all areas of being a managing director. We certainly would influence the vote of the sports club members.

5. Mary sells skincare and cosmetics.

She has no cosmetology certificate and no biochemistry background, but she wants to influence people to take good care of their skin. Mary decides to become a micro-expert in Botox substitutes.

Everywhere she goes, whenever she has a conversation, she talks about the alternatives to Botox. People then assume she is an expert in all areas of cosmetology. She has influence when she recommends her products.

6. Natural cold remedies.

When cold season approaches, many people get a cold. Sniffling and feeling miserable, they want advice on how to deal with the symptoms and feel better. If we become an expert on natural cold remedies, they will come to us. And now, they are more apt to take our guidance for all of their health issues.

7. Credit card advisor.

With one hour of weekly research, we keep up with the different credit card offerings. Some cards offer extra points. Some offer cash back. Some have low fees or no fees, while others have high fees. When someone wants a credit card, they don't want to do all that research. If we are known as the credit card expert, guess who they will come to for advice? And will they take our recommendations and guidance? Yes.

We create our influence because we have more information than they do. All we have to do is talk about the most recent credit card offering that fits their needs. People will notice. When it is time for them to want another credit card, they will come to us for advice. And who knows? Maybe our influence will spill over to other financial advice.

The human assumption.

If we are experts in one tiny area, people assume we have expertise in other areas. This isn't true, but it is the reality of how people perceive us. If we want respect from others, an easy way to do that is to become an expert in something. Anything.

Becoming a micro-expert can be better than becoming a general expert. It is easier to do, and it is easier to describe what we do.

Check out some videos on the Internet. There are many micro-experts with huge followings. That should be a clue for us. Becoming an expert in anything helps us acquire more influence with others.

When we are a micro-expert, we have a smaller audience. But we will have better influence with this smaller niche audience. They want our specific expertise.

Think of it this way.

When our computer is broken, do we want a famous movie star with wide influence? Or, do we want a computer geek with specialized knowledge that knows how to get our computer running again?

We will get respect and influence as a micro-expert.

CREATING INFLUENCE: STRATEGY #6.

Become a trusted advisor.

This is different than a salesperson attempting to sell to skeptical prospects. People anxiously await wise advice from a trusted advisor.

If we want others to perceive us as a trusted advisor, we need two things:

1. Trust. In earlier chapters of this book, we learned the basics of getting rapport and trust.

2. Advice. Because we are micro-experts, our advice must be better than the advice that our listeners can get elsewhere.

What happens when we become a trusted advisor?

Not only do people anxiously await our advice, they want to take action on it. They tend not to question us or hesitate. Instead, they look inside themselves and see if now is the right time to act on what we suggest.

We don't have to struggle to sell our ideas. People feel good about our suggestions.

But how will we get trusted advisor status with people who don't know us?

Tell people something they don't know.

What if people don't know we are a micro-expert? Or what if we are not a micro-expert yet? How can we still impress people so they give us their respect?

Salespeople can impress buyers with facts, figures, features, and benefits. But what creates the ultimate impression?

When a salesperson tells the buyer about a problem the buyer has, but the buyer didn't even realize the problem existed.

These salespeople appear to have superior knowledge. This act also shows concern for the buyer's situation by pointing out an unrealized problem.

When salespeople do this, they create respect and influence. Now they can influence and guide the buyer to better solutions for the buyer's problems.

Some examples.

Imagine we are a micro-expert on adding fiber to a diet to help people lose weight. We tell our friend that some types of fibers may be counterproductive. Our friend stops and thinks, "I didn't know that. I better take advice from my friend, the expert. I want to buy the right kind of fiber."

Imagine we were a micro-expert on children's reading programs. We could say, "Most accelerated reading programs give our children bad reading habits that will hold them back in the future. This reading program addresses their brains' comprehension habits, and also helps with comprehension."

What would the parents be thinking? "Wow, we don't want bad reading habits for our children. We better take this micro-expert's advice."

What if we were a micro-expert on building materials? We could say, "When we are looking for the right material, we also want to be aware of the effects of acid rain in our area." Well, if the buyer hadn't thought of this acid rain factor before, the buyer is impressed. We increase our influence.

If we become micro-experts, we will know specific things people should look for that they are unaware of now.

To create influence faster, we should make a list of problems or statements that will amaze our audience. When we tell them something they don't know, we gain the influence we want.

CREATING INFLUENCE: STRATEGY #7.

Become a celebrity.

Hard to do? Well, someone has to be famous. Why not us?

We may not become a movie star or a rock star, but we could become a celebrity in a niche. What niche?

When we become a micro-expert, there won't be much competition to be a celebrity that everyone knows. Okay, maybe we become a micro-celebrity, but we still are a celebrity.

Think about a movie celebrity.

A celebrity wears a pair of overpriced blue jeans. Will others want to follow her example, take action, and wear overpriced blue jeans? Yes.

Does she have influence? Yes. Is her influence deserved in the clothing market? Possibly not. This celebrity might be an expert on acting, but not an expert on the quality construction and design of jeans.

Remember that if we are good in one area, people will want to assume that we will be good in other areas too.

The famous retired sports athlete.

He received 22 concussions in his long career. Now he endorses a nutritional supplement. Will other young, aspiring athletes buy this supplement? Yes.

Does this retired sports athlete have influence? Yes. Is this influence deserved? Probably not. Do we want to take our nutritional or medical advice from someone who suffered 22 concussions? Sounds ridiculous. But, because he was a great athlete, we assume he is an expert in other areas too. And he influences others to try the nutritional supplement.

The retired politician.

He endorses a canned soda drink for retirees. Will some retirees take his advice and buy this soda drink? Sure. But is this retired politician an expert on soda formulations? Not a chance.

But because the retirees respected him as a politician, they respect his endorsement for a canned soda drink. He has influence.

But I am not famous for anything!

We can create our fame. I have a friend named Lisa.

Lisa runs for political office in her small town every election. She never wins. And I don't think she wants to win. But it only costs a few dollars to register as a candidate, and she gets free publicity every time.

Even the newspaper interviews her about how many times she has run as a candidate.

Now, who is famous in her small town? Lisa!

When she talks to people about her business, everyone feels they already know her. She is famous.

All it took was a few dollars and a few minutes to register as a candidate in the elections.

Could we create our fame by organizing a local charity? Or taking over an existing high-profile project that needs a volunteer leader? Yes.

With a little imagination, we can be micro-famous in our chosen niche.

CREATING INFLUENCE: STRATEGY #8.

Use word phrases that impress our listeners.

When we can read minds, we impress our audience. This gives us more influence for our message. Is it hard to read someone's mind? Not at all. Most people think the same.

Imagine we present to a hostile group. They lean back in their chairs, folding their arms, and no one is smiling. Yikes! They've prejudged us already, and we haven't even reached the podium yet. This looks ugly.

The first thing we must do is take their minds away from judging us, and get them to think about something else. The conscious mind can only entertain one thought at a time. Unfortunately, right now their thought is, "Okay fast-talker, what are you going to try to sell me now?"

This is not a good start if we want to influence people with our ideas or prompt them into action. Let's take their mind off us, and off judging us, and have them think of something else.

We will start our speech to the group with opening statements such as these:

1. "You are probably thinking…" Next, all we have to do is mention the obvious. We could say, "You are probably thinking, 'How long is this meeting going to last?'" The audience will think, 'Yeah. That is exactly what we are

thinking. You understand us. We think the same. I'll listen to what you are going to say next.'"

2. Or, we could start by saying, "If you are like most homeowners, you wonder, 'How will we get the money to fix these problems?'" And now their thoughts are on the budget, and not judging us.

3. Or we can start by saying, "Most people here tonight made a decision to take action instead of staying at home and watching television." Now our previously hostile and skeptical audience is thinking, "Yes, that is me. That is why I came here tonight."

4. Or we can start by saying, "As many of us know, the school budget isn't enough for the influx of new students." And our audience begins to nod in agreement.

Reading minds.

By mentioning the obvious, people think we have high-level, alien mind-reading skills. Impressed by our superpowers, we gain some influence.

But what if we guessed wrong? It can happen. But by mentioning what we thought they were thinking, many people will begin to have these thoughts anyway. Again, we accumulate influence so people will hear and act upon our message.

Could salespeople use these techniques also?

Of course. A simple example would be a salesperson saying this to the buyer: "If you are like most buyers, the first question in your mind is, 'How much is this going to cost me?'" This opening statement increases the salesperson's influence. It shows that he understands the buyer, and the buyer's problems.

It only takes a bit of empathy to imagine what other people are thinking. If we take the time to care, this is easy.

CREATING INFLUENCE: STRATEGY #9.

Use a structured sales presentation.

Influence helps us guide people to better ideas and better solutions. As we accumulate more influence, we build a more receptive audience.

Let's consider what people want. Do they want to talk about how our solution will work? No. It is important, but is not what they want. No one really wants to buy a solution.

So what do people want?

The outcome.

They want to know how things will be in their lives when everything is fixed from our proposed solution.

Since our audience is impatient, we shouldn't spend a lot of time talking about our great solution. Instead, we should spend more time talking about the outcome that our audience wants.

Here is a guideline for selling our ideas to others.

This basic sales formula is easy to follow and remember when we talk to others. It is not the only sales formula. However, it helps us focus on what our audience wants.

The sales formula.

1. **Here is your current situation.** Describe the problem to make sure we all understand the same problem. We want our audience's agreement on this problem. This helps make the current situation very clear in their minds. There is no need to propose a solution when the audience doesn't feel that they have a problem.

2. **Here is what you want your future to be.** Describe how life will be after this problem is fixed. This is what our audience cares about. They see the movie of the outcome in their minds.

3. **Here is how our solution will help you get to the future you want.** When we have influence, this part of our presentation will be quite short. They want us to guide them through the solution quickly.

Let's do some examples of these three steps.

1 Our skin wrinkles rapidly after age 40. It won't get better on its own. In fact, it will get worse.

2. You want your skin to look young and healthy all your life.

3. This skin serum protects your skin from the effects of aging. Simply apply it morning and evening.

Pretty simple. If we have influence, we wouldn't have to explain the ingredients of the skin serum product. Our prospect would respect our guidance because we have influence.

1. Our children's reading comprehension scores are falling. We don't want them to have low grades. If they have low grades, they won't have the education or good job opportunities they need in their lives.

2. We want good grades for our children. Then they can qualify for scholarships and apply to prestigious colleges and universities. Now they will have great job opportunities upon graduation.

3. I did an exhaustive investigation of the 20 top reading programs. Here is the reading program I recommend for our school board to adopt.

We are the micro-expert. No one else has thoroughly researched the 20 top reading programs. We established our credibility and influence. The school board wants to take our guidance.

We can even use this formula on our family vacation.

1. I know everyone is starving. But, it is late at night and few restaurants are open in this vacation resort.

2. But no one here wants to go to bed on an empty stomach. We are on holiday. We want to enjoy ourselves.

3. Fortunately, I went online before we left home. I made a list of restaurants that would be open after our late arrival. Here are the top three restaurants I picked.

The family thinks, "We have no idea where to go to eat. But we are hungry. You can solve that problem. Take us to the restaurant of your choice."

Let's break down this formula and look deeper.

This is a great formula to use because it is simple to remember. Later, we may want to create more advanced formulas, especially if we are in the sales profession. But for now, this will be better than 99.9% of our competition. Speaking clearly in a logical pattern impresses people.

Step #1. Here is your current situation.

Describe the problem to make sure everyone understands the same problem. We want agreement on this problem.

This step is where the hard work is done. Change takes effort. No one wants to change unless their current level of pain is high. It is easy for humans to tolerate low levels of pain and avoid the effort of fixing their pain. Here are some examples.

A. The squeaky door. Yes, we noticed the door squeaks. Will the problem go away on its own? No. But we can tolerate the squeaking sound for now. We put off fixing the door as long as possible.

B. The dirty car. Yes, we should take time out of our busy day to wash our car. But it doesn't look that bad yet. We will wait until the car is so dirty that we are ashamed to take it out in public. We have so many other tasks that feel like higher priorities.

C. That pile of paperwork at the office. It is a boring job to sort through all that paper. What do we do? We put it off. We delay until there is no more room on our desk. Or, we delay until the boss asks us if we finished the paperwork. Not finishing the job could be painful, depending on the attitude of our boss.

D. Cleaning and organizing our home office. Yes, sometimes we can't find things. But it is not that bad yet. To us, it would feel worse to spend hours of time sorting, filing, and organizing everything. So what we do? We keep piling notes, paperwork, drinks and random items in our home office.

E. The corner of our house needs to be painted. Yes, it is only peeling a bit now, but getting a ladder, a can of paint, and spending part of our weekend painting the corner of our house doesn't sound like much fun. Why not wait a few months until more areas of the house need paint? Then the effort seems worthwhile. We will wait until the problem gets worse before we take action to fix it.

F. The mole on our back. When it is small, no problem. We don't even worry about it. Sure, we should schedule a doctor visit and check it out. But that means fighting traffic into the city, taking off from work, and the mole doesn't feel that bad. Like most humans, we will ignore the problem.

As we can see, unless problems create more pain than the effort needed to fix them, the problems will remain.

Let's add some pain to these problems.

A. The squeaky door. It makes noise, and it looks like we don't take care of our home. Our in-laws are visiting this weekend. We want to impress them, and don't want them to think that we don't take care of our home. So we decide that now would be a great time to fix that squeaky door.

B. The dirty car. The receptionist tells the doctor, "Your car is filthy. Not only does it look terrible, but it reflects on this clinic. People might think we don't wash our hands between patients."

The doctor decides now is a great time to organize a carwash for her car.

C. That pile of paperwork at the office. On Friday, we get our annual job review. Not getting a raise this year could be disastrous. Since we don't want to look like an apathetic employee, we eagerly review and file the paperwork on our desk.

D. Cleaning and organizing our home office. It is nice to have a workspace in our homes. But it looks like a depository for clothes, sports equipment, shoes, and the occasional leftover pizza box. It is time to do our annual taxes. We can't find our receipts or tax records. In a panic, we start cleaning and organizing our office in a frenzy.

E. The corner of our house needs to be painted. At our local community association meeting, a neighbor tells us that we have peeling paint in the corner of our house. Then, our neighbor says, "I had that same problem. I didn't fix the corner of my house right away, and my house became infested with termites. It took us over $25,000 in repairs before we could eliminate the termites. That is a lot of money." After the community association meeting, we grab a ladder, paint can, paintbrush, and we are a mission to maintain our house.

F. The mole on our back. It is not a big problem, so we ignore it. Then one day, the mole becomes inflamed and our entire back feels like it's on fire. Do we feel the motivation to visit the doctor? Of course we do.

Describing problems clearly and dramatically is not enough. There must be motivation for people to invest the effort to change. Our audience needs to be aware of the problem, and we must raise their level of discomfort. We want the pain of keeping the problem to exceed their desire to not change.

There must be motivation to take action.

The first step is the hardest. We clearly describe the current situation, then add enough pain to spur action. This step takes the longest. But if we get Step #1 right, the rest is easy.

Step #2. Here is what you want your future to be.

Describe the situation after this problem is fixed. This is what our prospects care about most.

Step #2, what they want their future to be, is easy. All we have to do is to mentally take them into the future. Then we will describe life without that problem.

This step is fun. We help people visualize a better future without the pain of this problem. How will we know what that future will look like to them? Well, we could ask.

It could be as easy as saying, "So what would life look like if you didn't have that problem?" Or, "If we could get rid of this problem, what would you like to happen next?"

Humans have imagination. It is easy for us to think about a better future. If we are good listeners and ask the right questions, people will tell us exactly what they want their future to look like.

Then we will repeat this future back to them so it will be clear in their minds.

A great way to do this is with stories. Stories bypass the negative filters we have as humans. Stories help us bypass the salesman alarm, the too-good-to-be-true filter, the what-is-the-catch program, negativity, skepticism, etc.

Here are stories about the future for our six examples.

A. "Once we fix the squeaky door, everything else should look great. When the in-laws enter our home, they will smile. When they see how good our house looks, they will think we have the five best-behaved children in the city. I can't wait for them to come."

B. "With clean cars, when our patients come, they will feel confident that we pay careful attention to detail. They will want to receive their healthcare here. And we will feel proud about how this practice looks."

C. "When you go in for your raise, you will beam with confidence. No backlog of work, no unfinished business. You will appear to be the ideal employee that takes responsibility."

D. "With a clean office, getting our taxes finished will be a breeze. We won't waste time searching for scraps of paper. No frustration, and a great feeling for the rest of the year."

E. "We want our house to look great so we feel proud to live in our neighborhood. Plus, we will keep the termites away. Then we can relax and enjoy life without worrying about that corner."

F. "Once Dr. Alice looks at this mole, she will give you a little shot for the pain and remove it immediately. You will go back to feeling better. No more nagging worry that this could be serious. You will be back to watching your favorite TV shows without distraction."

Bottom line? Make the future without the problem look bright.

Step #3. Here is how our solution will help you get to the future you want.

"Let's do this now …" is a great way to introduce the solution. We didn't say that we will personally do everything to fix their problem. We will involve them in the process. It doesn't feel like we are telling them what to do.

Let's think about the people we are trying to influence at this moment.

First, they know they have a problem. This problem is painful and they want to fix it. They have the motivation to move forward. We made sure this was in place before we continued with our presentation.

Second, they clearly see that life will be better if they fix the problem. If there is doubt in their minds that the problem cannot be fixed, no worries. We remove that doubt now. People frequently know where they want to go, but they don't know how to get there. If we have influence, they feel relieved that we have a plan to get there.

We explained the problem and the solution clearly. This gives us influence. The final step is quick and easy. All we have to do is show them a way to fix the problem that gets them to the future they want. Let's do some examples.

A. "So let's do this now. I will go to the hardware store, ask the professional there if I need to buy an inexpensive oil to lubricate the hinges, or if I need to buy new hinges. Either way I will come home with what I need to fix this squeaky door. This shouldn't take too long."

B. "So let's do this now. You have patients booked for your entire day. I will telephone that high school kid who comes to parking lots and washes cars for busy people. I will ask him to come as soon as he gets out of school. Then I will set up a weekly visit. Done."

C. "So let's do this now. That pile of paperwork on your desk looks nasty. If we both work on it, we will finish it in two days. This puts me behind on my personal projects, but you can help me out after you get your annual job review and your big raise."

D. "I can't even organize the alphabet. But your friend Sandy at work is the world's greatest organizer. If she sorts things into files, I can take over from there. Let's call Sandy now. I will offer to take care of her lawn while her husband is away for three weeks on business. Then we can do our taxes in record time."

E. "So let's do this now. Call my brother-in-law. He has a ladder and is pretty handy. Tell him to bring his ladder on Saturday morning, help us paint the corner of the house, and I will send him back with a case of beer. How does that sound to you?"

F. "Let me call Dr. Alice now to get an emergency appointment for tomorrow. Then we will never have to deal with this mole issue again."

As humans, we have millions of bits of data bombarding our minds every second. We can't pay attention to everything. Our subconscious mind makes judgments for us. This sales formula sounds great to subconscious minds.

In this three-step presentation, most people will think, "Yeah, I have that problem. And yes, it would be great to live without that problem. You seem to have a solution all figured out. And wow, you presented it so professionally, without any hesitation. You have superpowers. I don't need to waste any brainpower on this. Let me use my limited brainpower to focus on other issues. I feel good now and I respect that you will sort this all out."

We create rapport with people. Then we propose a solution with this three-step presentation. They have feel that everything is okay, and that we are in charge.

We have influence.

CREATING INFLUENCE: STRATEGY #10.

Empathy.

As humans, survival is our #1 program.

We don't want to die. We protect ourselves. We think about ourselves first.

Yes, humans are selfish. Our wants, needs, and problems dominate our thinking. We think about ourselves all day long.

When we talk to people, who do they think about first? Themselves. Definitely not us. And certainly not our ideas or messages. Let's look at some typical thinking.

The funeral.

A good friend calls us and says, "My spouse just died. The funeral will be on Thursday."

What reaction comes to our mind first? Our calendar of appointments. We think, "Oh no. I will have to move my golf date and reschedule my nail appointment."

We shouldn't feel bad. Our survival program takes over before we have a chance to think. After a few seconds, our manners take over. We pass on our condolences and say how badly we feel.

The party.

At a party, we introduce ourselves and say, "Hi. My name is Chris. What is your name?"

Our conversation partner replies, "Your name is Chris? Chris starts with the letter 'C' and my company starts with the letter 'C.' Let me tell you about my company and my company's products."

Groan. A social evening ruined by a self-centered salesman who wants to pitch his goods.

The salesman didn't care about us or our name. The salesman ignored everything and only looked for an opening to start his sales presentation.

The gift.

Johnny and Cathy receive surprise gifts from Grandma. Johnny looks at Cathy's gift and complains, "Cathy's gift is bigger and better than my gift. It isn't fair. My gift should be better."

Johnny isn't thinking about Grandma or Cathy. Johnny's concern is getting more for himself.

"What is in it for me?"

Events are neutral. We can't control most events.

However, we can control our reactions to events. We determine our feelings toward the events. Consider the following events. Can we imagine two completely different reactions to these events?

- A football game.

- An announcement that our best friend is engaged.

- The outcome of a political election.

- The announcement of the winner of an Emmy Award.

- A car crash.

- A political speech.

In each example, some people will be happy, others will be sad. Same event. Two different reactions.

We interpret events based upon our situation and our view of the world. No matter what happens, we instinctively think, "What's in it for me? How does this affect me?"

Conflicting viewpoints.

For instance, a group of homeowners meet. They want to create a small park for the children to play. But each homeowner first thinks about how this park will affect him. One homeowner might think this:

"This would be great for the children. It would get them off the street so I wouldn't have to drive so slow in the neighborhood. I hate it when they play ball games in the street and damage cars. And if the park looks nice, it might raise the value of my home."

Another homeowner thinks differently:

"I don't have children. Why should I pay for a park I won't use? Why not let the homeowners who have children pay for this? I already pay enough in taxes."

Another example?

We want a four-day work week. Our commute is brutal. To do this, we propose to our office, "Instead of an eight-hour day, let's work harder and have a ten-hour day. Then, we could work four days a week, and have a three-day weekend. Yeah!"

Who would disagree with this incredible proposal? Fewer days sitting in traffic commuting to work. Three-day weekends with the family. A more relaxed way to live.

This is our viewpoint based upon our current situation. But what would others think?

Mary says, "This would never work. I would have to get extended childcare. My daycare center doesn't stay open late."

John says, "Work even harder? And for ten hours? I already feel exhausted by the middle of the afternoon. I couldn't do this."

The boss says, "We must be open five days a week for our customers. Even if we rotated the days off, we wouldn't have enough staff to service our best customers."

And so our great idea dies at the hands of selfish people, who only think of themselves.

Empathy.

We want to develop empathy to increase our influence.

Empathy is the ability to understand how other people feel. We don't have to agree with their feelings or believe what they believe. We simply experience their feelings in our imagination so we can understand them.

People beg to be heard. No one listens to them. Their children don't listen to them, their friends don't listen to them, and even their boss doesn't listen to them.

If we listen to people, they feel that we understand them. This helps us communicate our message. If people don't feel that we understand them, they create barriers of resistance. Our message then falls on deaf ears.

Empathy is hard work.

It is easy to see everything from our point of view. There is no effort required.

It is harder to see everything from others' point of view.

Because so few people attempt empathy, people take notice when someone does. And that "someone" can be us.

What happens when we understand other people's issues, viewpoints, and circumstances?

Our chances of influence go up. Way up. Others instantly notice our tolerance of different viewpoints. They feel safe that their viewpoints and beliefs are heard and respected.

Irrational, idiotic decisions.

Do we ever look at other people and wonder, "What were they thinking?" Sometimes, the actions of others don't make sense in our logical world.

When people make irrational, idiotic decisions, we must remember that these decisions are rational and intelligent from their viewpoint. And now the effort to understand their views begins.

No one intentionally makes bad decisions. We make decisions based upon the facts we have at the time, and on our view of the world.

Earlier we saw conflicting homeowner viewpoints on building a park. We saw conflicting viewpoints on a four-day work week.

Let's use our empathy to acknowledge the viewpoints of others, and see how acknowledgment gives us more influence and a chance to shape their final decisions.

The backstory.

The easiest way to develop empathy? Ask for the backstory. This helps us understand other people's journeys in life.

If we were on a date, wouldn't we want to know the backstory of our dating partner? Of course. This helps us understand our dating partner's values and view of the world. One's backstory influences one's future.

For example, on the first date the lady asks the man, "So you say you haven't been dating anyone for the last five years. Why is that?"

The man answers, "Well, my prison sentence was originally 15 years, but they reduced the sentence because of prison overcrowding."

And then the man asks the lady, "You are very attractive. I can't imagine you being single. Why no husband?"

The lady answers, "Well, my last four husbands died mysteriously immediately after they bought life insurance. So, I am single at the moment."

Once we know someone's backstory, we can appreciate their decisions. If their backstory is radically different than ours, then we should expect them to make radically different decisions.

Remember, we don't have to agree with their view of the world. However, we should appreciate their view of the world because their past was different.

The fear of change.

When we make suggestions or try to influence others with our ideas, what do they think? Why do others seem to resist change so much?

Here are some of their thoughts when we introduce something new.

- "Why should I change? I don't know what will happen next."

- "If I do this, will others think I am a fool?"

- "Is this the best choice? Let me wait to see if there are other choices."

- "Is this guaranteed? What if it doesn't work out?"

- "Wouldn't I be safer if I just continue as I am?"

- "What will my spouse think?"

- "Is this too good to be true? Shouldn't I be a little bit skeptical?"

- "Is this person trying to cheat me?"

- "What will happen if this change goes terribly wrong?"

- "Will I look like an idiot when I try to explain this to my friends?"

Our survival programs tell us to be safe. Avoiding change is a safe strategy. With these questions in mind, now we can appreciate other people's strange views of the world.

Here is an example of appreciating someone's view of the world.

The computer purchase.

I look at laptop computers based on the specifications of memory, processing power, speed, and functionality. Yet, my friend chooses a laptop computer based on how cool it looks when he uses it. He considers his laptop computer to be a reflection of his lifestyle.

I need a lot of empathy and some tongue-biting just watching how he purchases his laptop computers. But because I don't judge my friend based upon my rational specifications, my friend grants me influence. My friend allows me to make subtle suggestions on his purchasing decisions. Why? Because he knows that I understand that he wants something that looks sleek and flashy when he carries it around.

What would be the worst thing I could do to ruin any chance of influence? You guessed it. Disagree with his view of the world.

Disagreement sets up walls of resistance. Pointing out mistakes makes this worse. Criticizing their feelings? Oh my, we are going down the wrong path here. Communication stops.

It is not a good idea to disagree with someone's view of the world. People get their views of the world honestly from their personal experiences. We should respect that.

We can create more influence simply by being a good listener. People feel that if we understand them, we will only make suggestions based upon their point of view.

How do we get people to feel that we understand them? By agreeing with their statements. When they tell us their problems, their dreams, and their motivation, a simple nod of our head may be enough to create influence. People like people who agree with them. They feel that we hear them.

Remember the homeowners who wanted to build a park for the children?

Let's use our empathy to acknowledge the dissenting points of view. Because we understand that people make selfish decisions, we will show that we understand them by including their viewpoints in our proposal. It might sound something like this.

"I propose that we turn the empty land at the end of our street into a children's park. This will cost each homeowner only a few dollars for some basic equipment. I know the homeowners with children are all for this idea. But what about the homeowners here who don't have children? Why would this proposal be good for you? First, we get the children off the street so you don't have to drive so slowly to leave the neighborhood. Second, you hate it when the children play ball in the street and scratch or damage your car. And finally, with only a few dollars invested in basic playground equipment, we turn the vacant land into a children's park. This will increase the value of everyone's home. And we all care about the value of our homes."

Now the dissenting homeowners feel heard. They know that we considered their view of the world. Will our proposal pass? We don't know. But now we have a better chance than before. We used our influence, gained through empathy, to affect the dissenting homeowners' decisions.

What about that four-day work week?

Mary couldn't get extended child care. John felt exhausted by mid-afternoon and couldn't tolerate longer hours. And the boss worried, "I can't operate five days a week if everyone wants Friday off."

Well, everyone is against us on this proposal. We need to increase our influence. How? By acknowledging the conflicting viewpoints. People want to be heard. So maybe we'll adjust our proposal slightly.

"I propose flexible hours for our office. By working 45 minutes longer each day, everyone could take one full day off every other week. I know Mary worries about daycare for her children. But daycare is still open if we only work 45 minutes longer. And for Mary, one full day off every other week means she can go shopping during the week, instead of fighting the weekend crowds.

"For John, one full day off every other week means a full day at home to rest and recover from work. Wouldn't that be a welcome break? And John, I would suggest Wednesday as the day off. Makes the work week much easier.

"And I know the boss is concerned about the presence of a full staff to service our customers. Well, if we all made sure to take different days off, our office would be only one staff member short every day. That's the same as if someone was sick. But the good news is that everyone could use their day off to run personal errands, go to the doctor or dentist, and no one would need to ask for days off. Everyone would be happier."

Now, will our proposal pass? Maybe. But at least we have a better chance. We disabled the natural resistance of others by using empathy to address their concerns.

Empathy increases our influence.

People want to know that we understand them and see their viewpoints. To be effective when introducing new ideas or proposals, this should be our goal:

"Talk less about our proposal, and talk more about how our proposal affects them."

When we do this, we create influence and respect. Now others will hear us.

LET'S CREATE MORE INFLUENCE.

We now have a choice.

Instead of having our opinion ignored, we can influence people with our opinion.

Instead of feeling like a wallflower and blending into the background, we can confidently volunteer new ideas and proposals that can change people's lives.

Instead of feeling frustrated because others resist our great suggestions, we can now put our suggestions forward with the best possible chance of success.

Influence feels great. Now we can make a difference.

MORE BIG AL BOOKS

Quick Start Guide for Network Marketing
Get Started FAST, Rejection-FREE!

Our new team members are at the peak of their enthusiasm now. Let's give them the fast-start skills to kick-start their business immediately.

The Two-Minute Story for Network Marketing
Create the Big-Picture Story That Sticks!

Worried about presenting your business opportunity to prospects? Here is the solution. The two-minute story is the ultimate presentation to network marketing prospects.

How to Build Your Network Marketing Business in 15 Minutes a Day

Anyone can set aside 15 minutes a day to start building their financial freedom. Of course we would like to have more time, but in just 15 minutes we can change our lives forever.

How to Meet New People Guidebook
Overcome Fear and Connect Now

Meeting new people is easy when we can read their minds. Discover how strangers automatically size us up in seconds, using three basic standards.

Why Are My Goals Not Working?
Color Personalities for Network Marketing Success

Setting goals that work for us is easy when we have guidelines and a checklist.

Closing for Network Marketing
Getting Prospects Across The Finish Line

Here are 46 years' worth of our best closes. All of these closes are kind and comfortable for prospects, and rejection-free for us.

Pre-Closing for Network Marketing
"Yes" Decisions Before The Presentation

Instead of selling to customers with facts, features and benefits, let's talk to prospects in a way they like. We can now get that "yes" decision first, so the rest of our presentation will be easy.

The One-Minute Presentation
Explain Your Network Marketing Business Like A Pro

Learn to make your business grow with this efficient, focused business presentation technique.

Retail Sales for Network Marketers
How to Get New Customers for Your MLM Business

Learn how to position your retail sales so people are happy to buy. Don't know where to find customers for your products and services? Learn how to market to people who want what you offer.

Getting "Yes" Decisions
What insurance agents and financial advisors can say to clients

In the new world of instant decisions, we need to master the words and phrases to successfully move our potential clients to lifelong clients. Easy ... when we can read their minds and service their needs immediately.

3 Easy Habits For Network Marketing
Automate Your MLM Success

Use these habits to create a powerful stream of activity in your network marketing business.

Start SuperNetworking!
5 Simple Steps to Creating Your Own Personal Networking Group

Start your own personal networking group and have new, pre-sold customers and prospects come to you.

The Four Color Personalities for MLM
The Secret Language for Network Marketing

Learn the skill to quickly recognize the four personalities and how to use magic words to translate your message.

Ice Breakers!
How To Get Any Prospect To Beg You For A Presentation

Create unlimited Ice Breakers on-demand. Your distributors will no longer be afraid of prospecting, instead, they will love prospecting.

How To Get Instant Trust, Belief, Influence and Rapport!
13 Ways To Create Open Minds By Talking To The Subconscious Mind

Learn how the pros get instant rapport and cooperation with even the coldest prospects. The #1 skill every new distributor needs.

First Sentences for Network Marketing
How To Quickly Get Prospects On Your Side

Attract more prospects and give more presentations with great first sentences that work.

Motivation. Action. Results.
How Network Marketing Leaders Move Their Teams

Learn the motivational values and triggers our team members have, and learn to use them wisely. By balancing internal motivation and external motivation methods, we can be more effective motivators.

How To Build Network Marketing Leaders
Volume One: Step-By-Step Creation Of MLM Professionals
This book will give you the step-by-step activities to actually create leaders.

How To Build Network Marketing Leaders
Volume Two: Activities And Lessons For MLM Leaders
You will find many ways to change people's viewpoints, to change their beliefs, and to reprogram their actions.

The Complete Three-Book Network Marketing Leadership Series
Series includes: How To Build Network Marketing Leaders Volume One, How To Build Network Marketing Leaders Volume Two, and Motivation. Action. Results.

51 Ways and Places to Sponsor New Distributors
Discover Hot Prospects For Your Network Marketing Business
Learn the best places to find motivated people to build your team and your customer base.

How To Prospect, Sell And Build Your Network Marketing Business With Stories
If you want to communicate effectively, add your stories to deliver your message.

26 Instant Marketing Ideas To Build Your Network Marketing Business
176 pages of amazing marketing lessons and case studies to get more prospects for your business immediately.

Big Al's MLM Sponsoring Magic

How To Build A Network Marketing Team Quickly

This book shows the beginner exactly what to do, exactly what to say, and does it through the eyes of a brand-new distributor.

Public Speaking Magic

Success and Confidence in the First 20 Seconds

By using any of the three major openings in this book, we can confidently start our speeches and presentations without fear.

Worthless Sponsor Jokes

Network Marketing Humor

Here is a collection of worthless sponsor jokes from 25 years of the "Big Al Report." Network marketing can be enjoyable, and we can have fun making jokes along the way.

How To Get Kids To Say Yes!

Using the Secret Four Color Languages to Get Kids to Listen

Turn discipline and frustration into instant cooperation. Kids love to say "yes" when they hear their own color-coded language.

BigAlBooks.com

ABOUT THE AUTHORS

Keith Schreiter has 20+ years of experience in network marketing and MLM. He shows network marketers how to use simple systems to build a stable and growing business.

So, do you need more prospects? Do you need your prospects to commit instead of stalling? Want to know how to engage and keep your group active? If these are the types of skills you would like to master, you will enjoy his "how-to" style.

Keith speaks and trains in the U.S., Canada, and Europe.

Tom "Big Al" Schreiter has 40+ years of experience in network marketing and MLM. As the author of the original "Big Al" training books in the late '70s, he has continued to speak in over 80 countries on using the exact words and phrases to get prospects to open up their minds and say "YES."

His passion is marketing ideas, marketing campaigns, and how to speak to the subconscious mind in simplified, practical ways. He is always looking for case studies of incredible marketing campaigns that give usable lessons.

As the author of numerous audio trainings, Tom is a favorite speaker at company conventions and regional events.